out and back

Ptarmigan House
Maryland, USA

Cover design by Victoria Heath Silk (VictoriaHeathSilk.com)
Book design & typesetting by Studio26 (insidestudio26.com)

Out and Back: poems and reflections / Stewart Hickman. -- 2nd ed.

ISBN 979-8-9857393-0-5 (paperback)
ISBN 979-8-9857393-1-2 (ebook)

Out & Back
poems and reflections

STEWART HICKMAN

Ptarmigan House

To my mother,
Janet Adelaide MacMahon (1922-2006),
a gentle and discerning critic
since my earliest work.

To my sister
Martha Hickman Hild (1950-2024)
a listening ear, a fount of post-conventional wisdom.
Rest in Joy.

Contents

out

Autumn comes in parcels of trees

Autumn comes in parcels of trees
between the broad beamed buildings
to remind us of all autumns, memories
heaped like books about to
fall, all autumns that happened
effortlessly in parcels within
the blankets of noise and news:
the storms thrashing shorelines
down south, with missing people
(that soft sound, someone somewhere)
and strategy for the war beyond our shores—
softened before we hear it.
What gentler way to live than to delight in
the smell of soap on chrome, the skritch of rakes
on this leafy, peaceful ground?
So vast in memory. Stacked like books,
hemmed by what we build each year.

Flashes of insight

Watching lightning, a distant storm at night across a wide bay, each of us stood, amazed and awed, by the sudden illumination of whole banks of clouds by sharp, thick bolts. Two, then three, competing formations flash and parry, one to the northwest, one west-northwest, and one due west.

Our language contains imagery that links a flash of lightning and the impact of an awesome insight: "Then it struck me," "In a flash of insight," and the like.

In our watching, bayside, there are no blinding thoughts, only momentary blindness; no creative insights, only momentary sight afforded our far and tiny eyes. The mind, in fact, nimbly watching—here, there, over there, back here—anticipates the more miraculous, when tendrils of whiteness curl across the silent gray band of distance.

Later, on my camera, I will pause these flashes of sight and roll them back and forth, frame by frame: the lightning propagating out of darkness and going back into darkness. Back and forth I will spool and unspool the event of brightness, and slow down to a crawl that transition—in three seconds—from blinding darkness, to blinding light, and back:

> 00:00 Darkness, like looking into a pot of ink

> 00:01 A dim green miasma of rainy air, damp ground

> 00:02 Shocking brightness like a sun exploded, then leaves the translucent green of springtime, the lawn drenched in light, all detail clear, stunned, motionless

> 00:03 Darkness

There by the bay, standing still, we share a murmuration of amazement as our eyes recover from the insight. There is a shocking blue disk on the inner eye when you close it, which reminds your mind, with each blink, what it held for half a second. It's as though light bruises the retina. It's like new knowledge shocking the mind.

Enter servants, soldiers and attendants

I enter from the wings, leather cap
in hand; the room is packed with vital men.
One man, finds his light, and bears into his
Oratory, fills the sky with flakes
of speech, to pique his once-beleaguered foe,
pay homage to his lord, and so his strident
tone, a bell to some, to others, drone.

If there are no small parts in theater,
why am I here? I have no lines, I have no movement,
no attention rests upon my doing or my not doing.
I can hold my cap like this, or this.
Upstage right Messengers, Feather-bearers
Priests and I fill this mat of land,
bodies flaunting costumes on, then off.
There is no story in the thoughts we all hoard:
how lines, power, history accrue to few;
how most of human kind attend, add color, staging,
flurry, a mimic of the massive world, in this
small well-lit booth.
He's got as far as the line about the serpent's tooth,
portents, and fairer days, unbloodied rule,
that sort of thing.

Attend! Attend! We bend our gaze upon
the vital men, the scene at hand, duteous
to our cue:
            Yeoman, hither hie thee!
My Lord, I say, and, stage left, speed my leave.

The rest

In music, time is divided into beats; beats combine to form a measure of music, and measures are the building blocks of a composition. The music itself is a combination of notes (when some tone is created or sung) and rests (where there is silence). Some of the longest rests in orchestral music are given to the percussionists. Our musical effects—the striking of the tympani, a flourish on the triangle—are rarely sustained. For percussionists, there is a lot of nodding and counting until we reenter the aural landscape.

As the diminutive butler in a three-act community theater comedy, I had five lines, and, as soft-spoken father to the main character in an adaptation of a 19th century novel, I had only a few more.

A small role in a play is like being a percussionist in an orchestra: there is a lot of time to wait. In the comedy, I delivered a line about the book in the library, and then exited for ten scenes. My time in the backstage darkness was spent alone at liberty with my thoughts, listening to the roll of others' voices, others' speeches, until my next cue line—my signal to enter, cross the stage, pick up a spoon from the sideboard and utter my final line to Dimwick, the beloved yet clueless protagonist: "I'm told that the reaves have arrived, sir." It always got a laugh, even though we never learn what "reaves" are.

What if I broke the bonds of my script, and was, for once, the main action instead of the single line? One night, resting back stage, I ran through an alternative script in my head. I imagined my character, spoon in hand, raking his head left to right and bellowing, "The storm is coming, the quiet rage of death, and no life will be spared the felling." I saw the ensuing panic, actors stepping around the chaos I had made, to the delight of the audience, who didn't know this wasn't the way the play was supposed to end.

But I had second thoughts. How could I upend the art of my director and terrify my fellow cast members? After all, I chose to take on the assigned minor roles, full of rests.

Maybe, perhaps, my small role is like the passing geese calling from the cold sky. We hear them in the moment they wing through on their trek across the long, dark stage of night. Their voices are the essence of a perfectly delivered line, a measure of beauty in the silence.

So, I took my cue, delivered my line, and collected my laugh. Now, I regard the small role in a different light.

Strike the timbrel as though the angels themselves are listening for it.

Cassini

*"For thirteen years we just monitored and listened to
the data it sent back and I think that is the height of
human achievement."*
                    Linda Spilker, Cassini Project Scientist, JPL

Cassini, that metal pot,
explored the geysers of Enceladus,
passed over monstrous storms,
through solemn space,
ran out of fuel, and followed
the invisible arc of falling,
the losing battle with gravity,
a molecular pummeling
that ends with heat and the final light.

Someone listened and watched all those years.
Tell me, what do you see today?
Rivers of methane, delicate light.
The moons like tacks holding the parchment sky.
With what devoted tension do we listen
to our machines as they hold
forth hope against hope?
Listen, thinly, as they fall?

Direction

The medieval castle's outer wall has narrow windows, called arrow slits. They allow someone to see, but not be seen, to send arrows out towards an enemy, but not be struck by that enemy. The view is safe, but thin, and looks one direction only.

A turtle carries its shell behind. It's not in his way as he moves about the leafy forest floor, but he can't see behind it, save by turning—slowly—around.

We look at the stars, the light that emanates from them, the patterns they make; we focus less on the unseeable space between them.

A bowman, told an army is hurtling towards him, goes to his arrow slit, and devotes his attention to the narrowly defined task within the small visual arc of his purview. His comrades, left and right, see where he cannot.

Ever since the turtle turned, slowly, from the world to which he was headed, to see what is behind him, the world in front has changed significantly. Or not at all. He will not know which until he turns, slowly, back to his original trajectory, north-northeast.

There is an entire enterprise between two stars. I see one to the north; I see one to the northeast. The north-northeast is darkness. If my eyes could dive deeply enough, what would they spy?

Does all of what truly matters reside in the mesmerizing stars, the cardinal points?

What resides in the vast and disorienting dark?

Thought by the holly tree, sunset

What I feel I have
the Divine Author has provided.

What I have and know not that I have
the Author also has provided.

What I feel I lack, I might already have;
it may be given for me to discover.

I have nothing but what is given;
and nothing that is not given do I have.

What I lack, the Author has not provided;
perhaps denied that I might better see.

My envy, my sorrow, my yearning
might not render what I need.

But here by ancient tree, abiding sun,
sufficiency of sight.

The world I wake to

I wake up each morning to the world as I understand it. This is what I see: the benefits that accrue from qualities like peace and goodwill and generosity and kindness seem consumed by society's many failings. There are paths to greed and cash and ease and power that bedevil our efforts to keep light growing. Hope is beaten back, and any surplus of happiness is drawn inexorably down by the maw of war.

That's the world I wake up to, with no day measurably sunnier than the last.

But I, too, am a part of this world. Once, when I was making my usual commute to work, traffic slowed to a crawl and then stopped. "I hate this traffic," I thought to myself, staring at the mute and motionless bus in front of me. In that idling silence, it struck me. I *am* the traffic. I am in it, of it. I am the gridlock. I am the island of plastic floating in the Pacific. I am the post-industrial West.

That insight prompted reflection: Did I go wrong along the way? What path did I miss? Is it the way my carbon footprint breathes out more than my share of CO_2 into our thin shell of nitrogen and oxygen? Is it when I choose the fallow ground instead of taking on the full measure of my potential? When I take the route of petty sin, calling it "ease"?

How did I get here? I ask with feigned bemusement, because I know, well and full, how I got here; I walked every step, and felt, full and well, the impress of each footfall on the loam, saying to myself, "Here I go."

I wake up to each new day, I persist, like the world persists, a huge and heavy flywheel. I wake up many times each day—once to the morning window lightness, and again when I pick up something, anything, to take on. It could be work, it could be stopping to buy some flowers. In taking something on, I put aside some burden, perhaps: exchanging in a hundred ways what I take on for what I leave aside.

And go forward like that, as awake as I can be.

The nature of memory

It is time to fill these pages
in summer when all is lush
and full green.
Even then the snow cages hang
swinging in the trees
as birds bring brush
to the eves, and winter's moon
against the blazing blue
slides sightlessly into view.
It's a coming home, memory
brushing the green oak auburn
springing the gray back to green.
And found, sleeping at the
edge is a moss,
like a last lost word,
keeping its ancient shape
until we write it down.

Long coat

I'm walking at night with Sienna, my reddish-brown collie mix. Each encounter with the night exercises her eyes, ears, and nose. She is relaxed and alert to any movement, sound, or scent of interest. It's chill autumn, and I wear a warm black coat.

I remember, from decades ago, walking my boyhood dog, a Scottie. In those cool nighttime walks I felt in communion with God, or a god, one who liked to hear my thoughts. Now, I sense an old connection between that boy and the man I've become.

With my family, I attended a few marches, maybe for civil rights, maybe against the war. I felt an early tug to make the world better, more peaceful, more just. Yet I felt protected, too—under the mostly sunny suburban skies, against the dark and cold of the world outside, I wore a warm coat of privilege.

Now, older man, walking a younger dog, I feel that old coat and the blessings that hovered around it, and a great sorrow sweeps over me.

Maybe it is my friend's daughter who died recently.

Maybe it is Syria whose ruin I read about, gobsmacked: homo sapiens at their fiercest—the soldiers, the mobs of rifled men in jeeps, the airmen and their jets striking the hearts of houses—and humanity at its most immiserated, fleeing the places they fled to.

And yet I, we, moneyed, safe, with quiet streets, kind dogs, starry nights, eat well and can sleep in a state of blessed peace.

Large, white man, writing last poem

I am not Indigenous, First Nation,
nor Latinx, nor queer, nor of color.
I am not an other, rather:
Straight white male grey-beard,
majority, rule-maker:
keeper of capital,
the quo of the status,
the power of the structure
the we of the people.

The clear blameless white line of history is ours,
from Greeks to Anglos, to Pilgrims, to Pioneers
script by script writ for us, of us,
by us. (Bias. Bye, us.)

No tears but our own are cried for us,
the voice we had. And the
rights we claimed for us, piled high,
all will fall through this part of history,
selves which did not drown
from our wave hegemonic
will rise to the main text:
other selves, the once muted,
from the margins the marginalized, the
once under foot or foot-noted, the
undocumented peoples,
who take up the pen for the next
and already have

Shame

Even as far back as elementary school, 1963, Gerry made assertions that we all knew weren't true. Things like: "All stars are actually planets," and "The word 'few' means 3, and the word 'several' means 7," and "Paul is the only married Beatle" (it was actually John). He'd make these statements apropos of nothing, while we were waiting for the school bus, or outside at recess, whenever there was a crowd around. He was a scrappy, overly confident kid, tall, a good runner, used to winning. At the start of class one day, I challenged him, in front of the others, on the "all stars are planets" myth, and gently offered that there were only nine (at the time) planets that we knew of. His response was to make fun of how short I was, and the teacher told the class to get out our math homework.

I was embarrassed by the whole encounter. I don't believe Gerry was.

Later that same year, there was a footrace to determine who was fastest, an informal event in our neighborhood. The first time Gerry lost, he shouted, as he crossed the finish line behind another boy, "I wasn't racing!" He claimed he didn't know the race had started, and demanded a re-match. Losing a second time to the same boy, he accused an undefined "all of you" of cheating to make him look bad. An argument ensued. Gerry was called a "spoilsport" and a "sore loser," but he asserted his victory over those who would bring him down. Then some of us were called away for dinner and the scene dissolved.

I don't believe, to this day, that Gerry was ever embarrassed, by anything. But he was definitely afraid—fearful of being seen as wrong or foolish.

Scratch the surface of a tyrant, and there's a good bet there is a frightened Gerry, who has learned to say anything, and do anything, to avoid experiencing shame. Maybe the tyrant's journey begins with an early sting of humiliation. Torqued and wounded by shame, the young despot, who sees himself as wronged and cheated, perfects the art of demeaning the perceived enemy and holding his supplicants and followers in thrall of his righteous anger.

The problem is that Gerry grows into an adult, and the setting grows from a neighborhood to a community, a company, a congress, a command. The tyrant—and those who hold the bent mirror to his tirade—builds the case for action against any "other" —a person, a party, a publication, a tribe, or part of a sundered nation.

And through his guile, never stands alone.

The bass line

(for Larry B.)

we sing together like green
stands out against all winter—
the basso, below the blaze of sound,
tremulous, lone, steady,
and all else sings upon us—
the base from which
the grass unfurls
to the yielding and final
echo—like us—when song,
singing, both refrain.

It is then we hold the sorrow
the sheaves we mourn
and, hymn within our steady pace,
carry them the road home.

back

Beliefs: a sample

I

the universe has ended already,
and we are living in the echoes left over.
we believe this reality only because
we have never known the universe from which
these echoes propagated.
we are rolling to a stop.
the world we think we know
has come and gone,
foiling all fortune-readers, all fortune

II

the point of the universe is this moment.
the past is a ripple left over from ancient actions;
the future, unfathomable, a phantom.
we spend most of our time alert to shaken light and ghosts.
the moment—moving and motionless—contains
all grace, all gravity, all gratitude; it is
the only place to put our hands to work,
the only place to lay our heads.

The four signs

Poster board man plunked cross-legged in the sun, wearing someone else's suit and no shoes, says neutrinos will be our undoing and he gives a date, April 13, 2029. It is all explained, he says, in the tract of the ancient fathers of Moab. He preaches to the pavement and anyone in the right of way.

Something about knowing the truth that no one else knows animates his bright gray eyes and gives dance to his fingers that move through the documented litany of human misdeeds, like cadmium batteries, pet-owning, and sugar.

His treatise is written with a wide-nibbed pen on squares of cardboard torn from boxes. There are four squares, a gallery propped up by a rucksack or hung from a shopping cart. Left to right:

> You SAY the end of the world as we know it is yet to come. it is foretold in books, when all the horses escape; law and order falter; grids collAPSE; we hoard batteries, pencils, ice. locked in the promised apocalypse.

> BUT the world as we know it has alREADY ended. that ship has sailed, you are marooned have been since you were born. truth becomes tangled.

> The world as we knew it ended long ago that moment we stopped KNOWing it. so you can relax now. buy back stocks unbury your dollar coins. stop investing in avatars. trash the declarations for your communes of guns and goats.

The fourth sign, smaller in stature, written in a steadier hand, stands apart from the other missives.

GET TO KNOW THE WORLD AS YOU KNOW IT. Its whole folded intangible self is unfolding, like an endless fern, the fern of endless time is like an unfolding self, a self once wholly folded, completely untangle-able.

Most people don't pay mind. Some walk by in their tight shoes in the midst of a work day. Some are tourists looking at maps together. Many are lost in their phones. Occasionally, someone will start to read the four signs, but the gray eyes lock on them, and they move on as though being called away. A few people read the four signs to the end, where a watch draped over the edge of a metal cup sits on a card with the single word – WATCH.

A couple, holding hands as they read, now turn to walk, a recessional gait, as though a reverse thief had put into their pockets something wonderful, heavy, and full of gold.

Solace

(for my wife)

Where do we hang sorrow, in this rubble and doubt
with a world wretched with heat
and dust and wanting and
fear, a hungry dog that won't go home?

> You would say *There is a still sea of love,*
> *that we walk in daily,*
> *even if we grumble at its salt.*
> O, to be a man with head and with heart
> and strength to will forth great deeds!
> I tease out a splinter.

We fear the loss of wax and wane, what men have won
and lost a thousand times since he invented metal.
The moon has given up its place to smoke.

> Your sea of love is in each picture; we see it,
> by turns, as a flowing desert, ebbing marsh,
> bridge to somewhere.
> Can we sing again ever: *the sea of love is:*
> *there is no other where?*

Can you not understand this thing?
It is here on our oldest maps,
on our aging genes.
It hangs on men's unlistening hate.

> I always think of you as angel-like, even-footed,
> sweet-winged, humbled by earthly tasks. Our tools
> are wrong-handed for your trade.
> You are wanting a way to draw forth from
> the rubble of life some lilt to nourish,
> a way to help us listen to the sound of listening
> and a spoon to scoop the sea.

Life

On a distant planet called Tau Ceti-4, a microscopic fertilized cell, within the expectant mother, Azul, holds the potential of a live being. She and her mate, Bihan, are counting the weeks until their first child comes forth into this brilliant world, lit by two suns and encircled by three peach-colored moons. They have already picked out a name for their new child: Calla. They allow themselves to imagine a beautiful baby girl, with Azul's blue hair and Bihan's bright orange eyes. The sum of Azul and Bihan, however it is manifest, will come to light in nine months. But right now, the tiny cell, the ur-Calla, has all the code needed to miraculously grow and stretch to form Calla, unique and full of wonder and promise.

The inhabitants of Tau Ceti-4 share a deep reverence for life. Threaded through their literature, art, and philosophical writing is the theme of uniqueness of each member of the living community, the connectedness of all life, and the sanctity of that connection.

Parents the universe over feel their child is special and unique. Calla's parents, however, hold forth not only the uniqueness of their daughter, but the uniqueness of the histories that combined to form the cell that will become her. Tau Cetians think in terms of potential and probability, and express these ideas in ways that are once logical, naïve, and surprising. Here's how Azul, a mathematician and engineer, might think about it:

> The potential of Calla's code coming to life occurred during a window of time and a particular set of circumstances. That window of time is when Bihan and I are alive on the planet at the same time, both old enough to reproduce, and in the same proximity, to allow us to meet and eventually start Calla.
>
> The probability that her code could have occurred prior to us is zero; the probability of her

code occurring with only one of us is zero: the probability that her code could have been derived from any other two people, also zero.

Calla's life began at the beginning of that window: I was born in our year 734, and Bihan came along two years later, so we both grew to maturity around the same time. This new person, Calla, Life-willing, will be sustained by the deeds of many people and the protections, laws, and industries that arise to support the health and welfare of our civilization.

Life begins at the birth of the people who will make new life, and this has been the case since our origins. For any stream of wisdom and action, this is the fount.

Meanwhile, on another planet more like our own: in a city, in a battered apartment block, live expectant parents, A__ and B__. The neighborhood is where they grew up and where they met. A war has swept across the landscape, engulfing the city. The battle is ideological and political, and the outcome will determine which faction will rule. The conflict has caused tens of thousands of civilian casualties, including children. In violation of international law, the residential area of the city where A__ and B__ are now trapped is subject to mortar fire, day and night. Once a neighborhood of colorful, ancient marketplaces, it is now rows of rubble—dumbstruck apartment blocks, with windows gazing at nothing.

The situation in which A__ and B__ would bring C__ into the world is a window both narrow and fraught. Indeed, for the new life, C__, to take hold, a host of conditions have to be met. In the situation of war, the space of a world alive with potential contracts with each misery, and a future C__ approaches a vanishingly low probability, nearly inconceivable.

Tau Cetians appear to have answered in the affirmative the question, "Is all life sacred?" The answer is woven into the idea of being alive, a sense of being connected across geographical boundaries and through time. That no one shall take a life is a self-evident truth, as part of being alive as breathing, breaking bread, responding with empathy, listening to music, or watching the slow ballet of their peach-colored moons at night.

Tau Cetians have their fount of wisdom and action: the categorical protection of life. And the other planet, like our own, where countries are enmeshed in ideological conflict? Politicians and crusaders of many stripes decree the sanctity of life, but brooding over all is a belief in the rightness of deadly force to defend an interest and take up arms against each other. They speak of the inevitability of collateral damage, the justifications for war. Manifest destiny. The intent of their Creator.

Each crusade, each faction, with its own unassailable justification for death.

November song

When the autumn wind bends from the north,
the quick low clouds vex the laten sun,
the poplars stand sentinel over the ravine, and
the sudden just-cold teases your nose with the
notion of colder yet to come,
the presence of autumn, without words, without
nostalgia, only a great familiarity of reflection welcomed.
Fall back, says the old familiar force; it's colder now.
Time to find your place of warmth that says, so sharply
in this less forgiving clime, how blessed you are.
Pressing against an envelope,
some boundary closer than it's been.
Enter the grocery store, as the sun starts to touch
down through the scrim of tree lace at the horizon:
where else does life exist? Those unborn are waiting to enter, and
those departed are just that, gone.
The only inhabitants now are us, the shoppers,
until we find ourselves suddenly near the door,
pushing our carts toward the beyond, thinking
I thought this errand would take longer,
but here we are outside the Acme.
And it's over.

Privilege

Privilege is much in the news, as we deal with a national reckoning. Who has privilege and who doesn't? Is it earned or is it a right? Who or what is holding the current system in place? Can the system be changed to address disparities of access, wealth, ease of living?

The gradations of privilege have been depicted by some as a pyramid. At the top of the pyramid sit the "Privileged"—those not subject to the usual rules or limitations society imposes on its citizenry. At the bottom are the "Under-privileged," who are subject to more rules and limitations than usual. In the middle sit those who are subject to the usual rules and limitations.

Privilege does not confer to all. How can it? The word itself, like "height," requires, to have meaning, something called "depth"; "having," "not having"; and so on. The having of privilege implies a select group, the top of the pyramid, a privileged class, not subject to the usual rules or limitations.

The reality, right now, today, and for many centuries leading up to today, is that privilege accrues more easily to those like me: White, male, middle-class, educated, tall, abled, not young but healthy, straight, cis-gendered, Christian.

The moment I began confronting my identity—the sum of my heritage, my lineage from western Europe, my zip code, my orientation, my luck—was not a moment of pride or of shame. It was a moment of being more fully aware of my situation, and how different—how *so* different—life can be for another person; my neighbor, a fellow U.S. citizen, fellow human who is differently abled, neurologically diverse, nonbinary, struggling with debt, incarcerated, lonely, poor, abused, mentally ill, shunned, excluded, shamed, battling a war, or escaping one.

In this one life, I will probably never experience thirst, violence, discrimination, or homelessness. Though I see it happen to others, I'll never know it for me.

These days, many Chimeras slip their leashes and breathe fire upon the poor, the disenfranchised, the refugees, the exposed. But we who are not subject to the usual rules and limitations, not fighting to survive systemic violence, unrelenting poverty, or the murderous whims of a despot, can decide which monsters we battle, if we decide to battle any at all.

I march in peaceful protest without fear of being set upon by militarized police, shot at, or arrested. I have a voice people choose to hear, bland skin, and discretionary time. Admonished for speeding, I am given a warning and drive away with my life. My path is smoothed by inherited wealth. I am the beneficiary of a thousand pardons, a thousand second chances, and a thousand invisible favors.

Free from actual thirst, threat, poverty, or privation, I contribute my small measure of peace or counsel or solace to a troubled, broken world, and take pride in the value I add.

And with a mental jujitsu that I have had the privilege of a lifetime to practice, I ignore that little beast following me asking why I haven't done more.

O, funny bird, when I return

That nectar you wanted?
I had one tall glass,
long and light like the
long yellow line of
that southern sun
so thin across the
world of blue. I almost
flew with you, but did not.
We are like two halves of
the same word.
You come close to drinking
the sky when you launch
off the pebbly cliffs
as easily as I rise from my chair
but without the ache
and you sing as if one last chance
(though it is not).
Sitting back down, I'll watch you
when you split that
nectared light with your
firm unblinking wings.

Searching for good

I

There's a feedback loop from the very beginning when we look into an infant's face. I call her my "baby duck"; she smiles; I smile back; she moves her arm; I touch her hand. Each day awake is a big series of loops, as she figures out the world. Each day she is alert to surprises, searching for patterns and for novelty. Searching for good.

II

For decades, I taught classes on management and supervision; how to lead teams, how to give people direction and support, how to provide feedback. One day, a participant, a seasoned manager, asks this question: "What do I do with my poor performer?" There is a person who gets by on little effort, and who others on the team (presumably the good performers) have to "pick up after." Several in the class nod in agreement as if to say we all have poor performers.

My response doesn't occur to me until I say it out loud: "First of all, stop calling them poor performers. How you label them affects what you expect to see, and that affects what you actually see."

I walk over to the whiteboard and draw a loop, representing an interaction between two people.

"With your expectation of 'poor performer,' chances are you will be looking for errors. On the other hand, searching for good in them changes what you look for, which changes what you see in them, which affects how you treat them, which affects how they act, which, arriving back at the beginning of the loop, changes what you see in them."

That's what hope for someone is: it's a form of imagining a future for that person that creates a feedback loop in which that future is more possible.

III

Atmosphere and humanity form a loop, especially the troposphere, that thin band of nitrogen and oxygen, between 4 and 12 miles thick. This layer sustains us and all life, and, we are finding, it is sustained by us. Its character affects us—where we live, how we keep cool and hydrated, how we grow our crops. Our actions affect its character—witness global warming, attributed, in large measure, to our burning fossil fuels.

Searching for good involves searching for the connection and seeing if it is working to everyone's benefit. I look into my daughter's tiny blue eyes. We are creating a simple loop; I make a pop sound and her face brightens in one of those earliest smiles, the smile of a hundred joys, so I make another pop sound and she gives me another smile. I'm figuring out this newborn person; she is figuring out everything, one waking moment at a time. She will let me know when something is amiss, when she is hungry, wet, startled, or sad—cloudy for no reason I can tell.

I will go to any lengths to make it right.

Poetry after the fall

Being witness to people living
on haphazard stilts in metal huts
lining the black lake banks,
changes one in the gentlest of ways,
seeing where life can be put.

Verses of mine were frail crafted lines,
of gardens, and starlight, and hoot of owl,
before the fall of Aleppo, cruelty the
length of time drowning caravans of
lives, the quiet human howl.

Refugees on the soccer field

I stood on a small bridge over the stream with my dog, Sienna, and observed a mother watching her four boys build a pebble dam to divert some of the stream flowing over a flat area of rock. I told the mother that this is what I did all the time when I was their age. She said it was a kind of recess before going "back to class" at home. Back in the 1960s, Boulder Brook—an oft-visited stream in a neighborhood adjacent to ours—was as vital as recess to my pals. We diverted and re-diverted creek water for whole afternoons.

By the time Sienna and I reached Long Branch Parkway, I imagined an urban boy, same age as those four boys, deep within a city. In that setting, there is no stream making its way through a section of towering forest. This urban kid is miles from a forest. Has he even *been* to a stream? What is the ratio of boys who get to play in streams to boys playing on city pavements? Is my pastoral scene better? Why do I feel sorry for the imagined urban boy? I think like this for two blocks. We are now at the soccer field. There is a cool breeze in the late morning; the sun is slightly hazed by the jet stream carrying smoke from the forest fires on the west coast.

How many shelters would this grassy area contain if this soccer field and the surrounding lawn were a refugee camp? I estimate 120 tents. Take away the grass, turn up the sun, the wind, turn off the flowing water in the glen. Take away the shade, the tall green, the word "lush." Add a pandemic, add the hush of misery, counterpoint to everything I can see and feel here with my dog.

Does this leap of imagination serve a purpose? Is it an exercise of some deep moral muscle? Is it a way—my way—to stay in shape, to feel humbled by the abundance the world gives me without effort each day? To feel gratitude, to practice watching? And for anything watched—this quiet green field, for instance—imagine it gone, replaced by dust and rows of tents. Now bring back the soccer field. Now erase it. Now bring it back again.

Maybe this kind of imaging of the small bit of information I have about the larger world—keeping it in front of me—is creative. Or curative. Or maybe it's just another aspect of leisure that I can take or leave.

Back at my house, I let Sienna off her lead and she runs, I walk, up the steps to our shaded yard.

Sometime leave the shore

I will sometime leave the shore
as opposed to think about it, walk along it,
or dream out from it a new way to be.
I will leave land for the fragile sea.

The journey of each landward oak
is marked—the twist of the trunk,
the storm-broken limb—
It towers like a tree; it is misshaped by time.

At the point I trade rooted step
for salty brew, I will cease staring
at death, like a boiling kettle, wondering
when will it whistle for me, for you?

And when I do, say "this is I,
the whole might and break of me."
Instead of cloaking quiet fears,
cast them off, throw them over,

Set aside my limits even in this
time, with these very hands, so small
and say this, this is how I practice
what it takes to set a burden no one needs

Down. To arrive at a stepping off,
a journey now fully inhabited.
I can be more home, and maybe see you home.
And you, and you. There are so many of you.

When those stony hills welcome me

When those stony hills welcome me
I will know something of home;
it won't be like going back, rather
I will be fully awake, as though
the verse that I love were to
find me and come around me
as when you watch a single bird
then come to see two others watching
you; and before you know it
you are hung round with verse.
They are the lines that made you.
In that moment of being braced
by the stony hills, there is a moment
of completeness—not of a life complete
as though these rocks mark my rest;
rather of life completed in every moment—
coming to see people as they are and
have always been. I have yet to drive
to those stony hills, and when I get there
I will be neither the boy with boyish
temper; nor the man I momentarily am;
nor any of the long list of selves;
only this one man, stepping over
the net he never learned to cast,
stacking and restacking books,
grieving and laughing
and in grieving, laughing
a citizen of two worlds
but home here, these half-used hills
these rocks of former fences.

ACKNOWLEDGEMENTS

This work was drafted as part of the Creative Momentum Collaborative, a year-long online community of artists in the Washington, DC, area, convened and facilitated by authors Mary Amato and Diana Friedman in 2021.

Thanks to my early readers, Mary Amato, Martha Hickman Hild and Molly Graham Hickman.

Thanks to my editors, Greta Ehrig (poetry) and Jamie Holbrook (prose). Each of you has made a positive impress on this volume through feedback adept, encouraging and precise.

Thanks to my wife, Busy Graham, guardian of my solitude.

ABOUT THE AUTHOR

Stewart Hickman is a Maryland-based poet and essayist whose work explores the ambiguity and perplexity of human consciousness. A former high school English and creative writing teacher, he went on to spend four decades in organization development and executive coaching, working in international agricultural research, global non-governmental organizations, healthcare, charter school systems and USAID. His extensive experience in the "Majority World"—the 80% of humanity living on less than $10 a day—along with his deep engagement with organizational systems and dynamics, shape the humanistic and multicultural perspectives found in his writing. Hickman has served as a panelist for the Maryland State Arts Council's Individual Artist Award in literary arts, and his work has appeared in the Delmarva Review. He is the author of two chapbooks, *Out and Back* (2022) and *why i never got to neptune* (2024), and he publishes a weekly Substack, *Meanwhile, Elsewhere.*

More at:
StewartHickman.com | eshickman2@gmail.com

www.ingramcontent.com/pod-product-compliance
Lightning Source LLC
Chambersburg PA
CBHW030525130626
46549CB00007B/3107